Supernaturally Made: Reclaiming Your Eve
Vol. 1

DR. SONIA KENNEDY

Published by
Greater Working Women Publishing, LLC
www.gwwpublishing.com

Providing Publishing Services for Christian Authors & Organizations: Hardbacks, Paperbacks, E-Books & Audiobooks.

Supernaturally Made : Reclaiming Your Eve Vol. 1

Copyright © 2018 Dr. Sonia Kennedy

All rights reserved. Printed in the United States of America. No part of this book may be used or reproduced in any manner whatsoever without written permission except in the case of brief quotations em-bodied in critical articles or reviews.

ISBN: 978-1-948829-05-2

Second Edition: April 2018

10 9 8 7 6 5 4 3 2 1

TABLE OF CONTENTS

Foreword	i
Introduction	1
Chapter 1 Reclaiming Your Eve	5
Chapter 2 Rocking Your Queendom	12
Chapter 3 I Am A Divine Creation	17
Chapter 4 How to Get Everything You Want	22
Chapter 5 You are A Supernatural Investment	28
Chapter 6 Supernatural Success	36
Chapter 7 Self Love & Emotional Empowerment	40
Chapter 8 Your Identity	44
Chapter 9 Perfectly Imperfect	49
Bonus Chapter: From the Superpower Playbook	52
Supernatural Tools To Use	55
About the Author	61

FOREWORD

Hello Queen! Thank you for purchasing this guide for your empowerment. I wrote this guidebook initially to empower women to Go Beyond Their Ordinary Best and Live their Best Lives! What started out as a space for empowerment and influence for women has meta-morphed into so much more.

As a Success Coach & Therapist I work with clients to transform and ignite their mindsets, unleash their supernatural powers, show up fabulously, and get healthy, all while creating a life worth celebrating!

Before we get into the juiciness of being you, I want to express my deepest love, gratitude, and a heartfelt thank you to my Mother, my Superhero, J.D., for showing me it was okay to wear my cape and still be in my own feminine energy, to my Supernaturally Made Sisterfriends: the list is too long to name, but I so appreciate you for allowing me to be me and for sharing yourselves and your power with me. Shuntella Richardson, Success Coach and Supernaturally Made Diva, thank you for your mentoring and words of power. To Dr. Camille Quinn and her mother, Jessica for their unwavering cheers and words of encouragement, Camille, your mother is a true ride or die Queen! To all of the mini-Divas & future Plan A's that I have had the privilege of taking care of and loving on, don't ever forget who you are! To my Supernatural Success Coaching Clients, continue to use your superpowers to serve powerfully and play big in the world! To the Supernaturally Made women I have yet to embrace, I say a thank you in advance for the lessons to come!

Back to the Supernaturally Made public service announcement: I share my passage into womanhood and being Supernaturally Made because I want to be transparent in the quest of being a successful woman in today's society. Much of what we see via social media and other visual outlets don't show us the trials and tribulations of successful women leaders. This lack of transparency positions aspiring women entrepreneurs and leaders to strive for perfection at the expense of their emotional health and well-being. While Supernaturally Made, Vol. 1 calls women to celebrate their emotional empowerment, the truth of the matter is that we are forfeiting our ability to be feminine, to be adventurous, and to be tuned in to ourselves. We are looking for the fastest route for recognition and achievement rather than honoring our own special process. The jewels and gems acquired in our pursuit are overlooked in our desire to feel accomplished. As a result, more and more women are reporting periods of depression, struggles with anxiety, diminished social connections, and trauma related issues. This is a widespread cycle that women undergo as they struggle to claim their space in the Universe.

While there are several books that inspire women to be their best, I wanted to expand the space for women to own their legacy, to be who they really are, to do the work that needs to be done, and get what they want. This includes owning their right to participate in the world free of guilt, judgement, assigned roles, expectations, failure, deadlines, and comparisons-contributing factors to the pervasive perfectionism syndrome that women feel compelled to take part in. My giveback and service to the many women that struggle with these issues is at the heart of Supernaturally Made.

Do you or someone you know have struggles with uncertainty about how to get started on their goals or dreams and they want to take action? Are there feelings of uncertainty or doubt about you or their presence in the world? Give them this book as a gift. As a matter of fact, purchase this for your girlfriend circle or sister-tribe so that you can all hold each other accountable on your journey to being Supernaturally Made.

Want to have a conversation with me about being Supernaturally Made and your journey to emotional empowerment? You can reach me at facebook.com/empoweringwellness360 or my Instagram page: @YogaBodhi360. You can also follow me on my personal page at facebook.com/soniakennedy. Feel free to email me at drsoniakennedy@empoweringwellness360.com or via my website at empoweringwellness360.com

Until then,

Be Uncommon!

Dr. Sonia

INTRODUCTION

It is time Sis! Time to change the patterns in yourself and how you relate to you. You know you are destined for great things yet you keep putting them off. Statements like, "I'll do it when the kids are away at school, "I'll do it when I lose weight", "It's too expensive", or "I don't have the money," keep you hostage and stagnant. Yet that thing keeps showing up. You know that thing, the one that keeps you up at night-that keeps calling to your spirit, nudging it to action. It is not going to go anywhere, because it is letting you know it is time to get back to you. Otherwise, how can you relate to others when you cannot relate to yourself?

Imagine what it would be like to accomplish all your goals. To have a greater level of self-awareness, to leap problems in a single bound, be on time for appointments, maintain self-management and show up in the world in an energized and positive way! Supernaturally Made Vol. 1 is about Rocking Your Queendom, Getting What You Want, & Living Purposefully. This guide is the answer to your call.

This guidebook is for the woman who wants to have greater intimacy with herself in all aspects of her life-personal, career, business, social, physical, and spiritual. You are ready to dig deep and figure out what you need and how to put you first without feeling guilty or feeling like you are neglecting something or someone. You are ready to align your values with your lifestyle so you can stand out, play big, and turn up in the world! You want your giveback to be huge, right? You want the Universe to expand your Queendom? The only way to do this is to invest in yourself from a deeper level-a supernatural level.

What does being Supernaturally Made mean and how can you incorporate this in your life? Supernaturally Made is doing the uncommon and undergoing a transformation. When you are Supernaturally Made, you focus on the internal first, because you know healing starts within. You create a better life, beyond normal, so much so, that it is unordinary! You live your life on your own terms by awakening and activating both your mental and physical. You create infinite possibilities and learn how to be present in the moment. Being Supernaturally Made requires you to get back to a healthy space of balance. When you are Supernaturally Made, it means you have a new way of thinking, a new purpose, and a new outlook. Your thinking is full of powerful ideas that serves you and others in the world. Does this sound like you?

Throughout this guidebook, I will be asking you to make the commitment to you. You are the PRIORITY! Supernaturally Made Vol. 1 is the introductory guidebook to the Supernaturally Made series. It will require you to do some soul-exploration and me-flections to examine what you need more or less of in your life. It will also show you how to create a loving and purposeful space that allows you to rock your queendom as a woman of distinction, enlarge your territory and get what you want, and embrace your superwoman as a divine creation! I broke the book up into three sections: **1) Rocking Your Queendom,** covers Chapters 1-3, **2) Getting Everything You Want,** covers Chapters 4-5, and **3) Living Purposefully,** covers Chapters 6-7. Each section is a gateway that will allow you to embrace your path to being Supernaturally Made seamlessly and position you for your transformation!

Use this guidebook as a goal-setting tool to get you in action. The book has goal-setting questions to help you be intentional in identifying your strengths and areas for growth. There will be quotes and affirmations throughout the book to motivate you towards success and completion. There will also be tasks and challenges to complete as a part of your self-work. The questions at the end of each chapter will force you to challenge your thinking and do some paradigm shifts, as well as, listen to your inner self, but I know you are ready for the challenge! Otherwise, you would not have shown up! Are you ready for your supernatural journey of self-discovery? Are you set to take that one-step for change? Are you prepared to re-introduce you to yourself? Grant yourself permission and give your spirit what it needs so you can up-level and Go **Beyond Your Ordinary Best!**

Side note: I will use the words Universe, Creator, etc. and make references to Biblical characters in the book. This in no way reflects or is intended to persuade anyone's religious beliefs or denounce anyone for his or her respective positions. I am only speaking and sharing from my experiences and positionality, which is what lead me to write this book. It is my hope that that those who read this book recognize that transformation does come from within your soul center!

For the worksheets that accompany this guidebook, you can email me at drsoniakennedy@empoweringwellness360.com or via my website at http://www.empoweringwellness360.com

Trying to be everything to everybody can be both challenging and emotionally draining.

Chapter 1

Reclaiming Your Eve:

Being Supernaturally Made versus Superhuman

"Build a Queendom That Cannot Be Shaken"

Dr. Sonia Kennedy

People keep telling you to take off the superwoman cape. With a confused voice, you say, "Why, my cape allows me to be a great mother, wife, sister, best friend, lover, and pull off everything in between." I need to wear the cape or I will let everyone down." My superstar sister, what I am about to share with you is confidential and only available to women who are willing to be vulnerable, exposed, and live without restrictions.

Your cape was created for you by design! The problem is not that you wear a cape; the problem is how you wear the cape!

Trying to be everything to everybody can be both challenging and emotionally draining. We are caught on a constant spinning Ferris wheel circling between leading, having more things, being happy, and doing more. Any room for imperfection or realness to show up is smothered. Even though people expect you to be the leader, the problem–solver, the fixer, the one who has it all together, the truth is you are only HUMAN. This is the most important thing that you forget when trying to be everything for everybody.

One of the most prolific female authors that I most admire, mother Audre Lourde, writes, "If I didn't define myself for myself, I would be crunched into other peoples' fantasies for me and eaten alive." I remember reading this powerful quote and getting an "aha" moment. It was during the time I was competing in the Miss Chicago Pageant and not feeling sure or confident about my talent. At that time, they did not have a talent category for Game changer! Competition for beauty and talent can bring out our worst insecurities as a woman and make us doubt our abilities to perform as we are called. I knew that I was a woman with talent; I was just uncertain what value my talent had. I had not yet defined myself for myself. I had been conditioned to allow the world to define me and then to act accordingly to the roles assigned to me. This was my womanhood alert and a mission that needed to be completed.

Now, as a woman leader owning her various talents, where I am called upon to support and assist women in achieving their goals and dreams, looking back, I am humbly reminded that I am only human. The opportunities, knowledge, and wisdom, afforded to me, are all supernatural gifts and blessings. It was only when I stepped into womanhood, and owned my legacy as a blessing-outright declaring and reclaiming my Eve, was I then able to move with clarity, complete transparency, acceptance, awareness, perseverance, and commitment. That transformation was a 360 for me that I can now share with other women in a powerful way.

Ever been there? Not sure about your place in the world as a woman or what big dream you should be focused on? Or are there a ton of things you want to do, but someone else placed limitations on you, and you operated within them? We as women look for validation in the world, yet we must own that we are co-conspirators in our complicity to conform under notions of purity, weakness, submission, or obedience. We are told not to trust ourselves or other women, no matter what we achieve in the world. Just as I have been transparent with you in sharing my story, I want you to be open to your own process, for what I am going to ask you to do may be out of your comfort zone. That is okay. I want you to be uncomfortable. I want you to be so uncomfortable that you do something uncommon after reading this. This process is your Womanhood Renovation! You should be excited Queen! We are about to do a complete demolition down to the bare walls of our Queendom so that we can step into our greatness without fear, reservation, or hesitancy. I do not want you to be the woman who does not walk in her full calling because she allowed fear to speak louder than her heart!

Part of this Womanhood Renovation requires us to reference the first woman on Earth, Eve. I mentioned reclaiming my Eve as my entry into owning my talents and gifts as a woman. I know that this requires a deeper explanation where I must tell the story of Eve as woman. I will not re-visit the complete account of Adam & Eve here, but I will say that Eve continuously gets a bad rap, despite all of her accomplishments. No one can dispute that she was a pioneer in a world based on firsts. She was the first mother to give birth to a living breathing human. She was the first companion and partner to man. She was the first woman to walk the Earth. Was she superhuman? No, but she was definitely created by a supernatural force and with intent. We know that a "curse" was placed on Eve and her female descendants. This is sometimes referred to as "the curse of being a strong woman." This "curse" resonates with women even now at some venture of their life journey. Based on historical accounts, we also know that Eve was strong and a survivor. So why wouldn't her heirs have similar qualities and DNA? Much like I called my reclaiming of my Eve a blessing, we have to change the language from "curse" to "blessing" if we want to have a new way of being in the world, a new way of thinking, a new purpose, and a new outlook. These are the concepts of being Supernaturally Made.

Where do we start with being Supernaturally Made? Acknowledging how we have subjected ourselves to the notion of having to be strong or appear to be strong to be accepted as a woman is a beginning. Imagine Eve in her cape. I speculate she wore a beautiful cape of color with reds, golds, yellows, and oranges that was fabricated just for her. I believe it was a vibrant cape constructed to withstand challenges, to endure struggles, to share wisdom, and to create a world of love. It could not be anything but a supernatural cape and only a Supernaturally Made Woman could wear it. The Creator did not bless Eve with her cape to be superhuman, superwoman, or superman. She was simply a supernatural creation-a supernatural woman. Our cape, is our heirloom and blessing. It is passed down to us from Eve; therefore, it should be seen as one of power and resiliency to assist us in times of direction and difficulty.

<u>Reclaiming Your Eve Questions:</u>

How will you begin reclaiming your Eve?

What supplies/tools will you need to set yourself up to win?

What habits do you need to discard?

What practices do you need to begin?

What type of support do you need from your tribe/friends/family?

What will your future look like when you implement changes?

Task/Challenge: Create a brag list of your accomplishments. The list does not have to be extensive because you will continuously add to it over a period of time. I will give you a head start because you invested in yourself and your goals when you purchased this book. Carry this list in your phone and add to it regularly. Pull it out when you feel the need to compare yourself to others or when you feel that your pace is not fast enough.

Affirmations Just For You!

I am The Plan A

I am a Woman of Strong Power

I am Resilient

I will live in Powerfulness

Use the Affirmations listed above or create some of your own to assist you in your Supernaturally Made journey. Practice repeating them to yourself out loud for one minute. Pay attention to how your attitude and actions. Take it a step further and journal about the changes you notice. Embrace the supernatural person you are becoming and watch the universe open up for you!

IF NOT YOU THEN WHO?

Chapter 2

Rocking Your Queendom:
You Are a Woman of Unique Distinction

Now that you know who you are, have you ever found yourself trying to figure out why you are here? All of us as women have attempted to answer these questions and figure out our role. Given what we currently see in today's society, your identity could be submerged in an undercurrent of falsities that have you striving for perfection. This takes you out of your true calling to "Rock your Queendom", or what you would call, claiming your identity. I want to lighten your load and release you of that burden of struggling with who you are and collaborate with you so that you are showing up every day as a unique woman of distinction.

Author & speaker, Suzanne Burden, discusses Reclaiming Eve and gives us a snapshot of how the first woman on earth rocked her queendom as a unique woman of distinction: *"Women are a part of God's Plan A.... they are the perfect finishing touch...an agent of rescue who is suitable, strong, powerful, intentional, and purposeful."*

Wow, Diva! You are a Plan A! The first plan. A Queen in a Kingdom. Suitable, Strong, Intentional, and Powerful. Not a second plan, temporary band-aid, or quick fix. You are a product of a divine creation based on your lineage and connection to Eve. If she was the one and only plan, then so are you. There is none other like you. Your rareness is what sets you apart as an original model. You are not just the "help." Burden goes on to say that women are not just "domestic servers and that (domestication) is not our primary identity." This is huge because we cannot rock our queendom and live as we are called to in all of our fabulousness because we are struggling with our identity and place in the world. You know those teachable moments that were painful and felt unbearable? The lessons learned? They help you connect with your queendom outside of the roles of mother, sister, wife, etc. They assist you in claiming your identity in what Burden refers to as an adviser, agent, lover, rescuer, and mentor. Like Eve, there are even more identities because of our uniqueness: revolutionary, disrupter, and adapter.

How you see yourself in any of the roles above or with other labels, through loving or critical lenses, determines how you approach and ultimately "rock your queendom"- live your life. While this may be a complex concept because of your previous thoughts, attitudes, and feelings, you are equipped with the power to use all of your uniqueness to supply the world with what it needs from you!

Rocking Your Queendom Questions:

What supplies/tools will you need to set yourself up to win/Rock Your Queendom?

What is that one thing that <u>only you</u> can bring and deliver to a situation?

What habits do you need to discard?

What practices do you need to begin?

What type of support do you need from your tribe?

What will your future look like when you implement changes?

Task/Challenge: Create your Plan A goal list. Try creating categories for family, personal, career, business, spiritual, and fitness. What will be your firsts? Where are you spending the most time? Where do you need to balance your time? When will you celebrate your accomplishments?

Affirmations Just For You!

I Operate in Full Authority

I will venture into new pathways

I Will Be Audacious

Use the Affirmations listed above or create some of your own to assist you in your Supernaturally Made journey. Practice repeating them to yourself out loud for one minute. Pay attention to how your attitude and actions. Take it a step further and journal about the changes you notice. Embrace the supernatural person you are becoming and watch the universe open up for you!

THERE IS NO REWARD FOR JUST FITTING IN!

Chapter 3

I Am A Divine Creation:

Being Unordinary, Uncommon, Unbeatable & Unbreakable

"Your Attitude Determines Your Access"

Dr. Sonia Kennedy

Now that you have reclaimed your Eve, and you know that you are the Plan A, and your thoughts have experienced a womanhood renovation, a new and divine creation has emerged. This Divine Creation is one who is strong, fierce, intentional, and filled with purpose. You are dialed in and directly connected to your Supernaturally Made Woman. Hats off to you Diva! You are prepped and set to make your passage gracefully into Living Purposefully. You know that your pedigree is filled with unordinary talent, uncommon plans, unbeatable strength, and unbreakable resiliency. Will there be a time when you show up and you may have fear or setbacks about being judged, isolated, or retaliated against for your confident walk into woman-ness? Yes, for sure! A Divine Encounter will assist you in your transformative process. All you need to do is evoke your supernatural cape!

To help you through those times where you forget to put on your cape, follow the model for the **Fingerprints of the Supernaturally Made Woman:**

A Supernaturally Made Woman has:

1) **Uncommon Thoughts:** her thoughts are not normal, regular, or standard. Her frequency may even be different in terms of how she creates ideas.

2) **Uncommon Plans:** her uncommon thoughts turn into uncommon plans. Her designs and plans are beyond the average and ordinary. She is urgent in her approach from concept to completion.

3) **Uncommon Discipline:** her mastery of self-regulation allows her to show up consistently ready and on point! Her plans are implemented and in working order.

4) **Uncommon Vision:** her dreams are constantly enlarged; she feeds her tribe and blows through any obstacles that may halt her ideas from coming to fruition. She does not hesitate when her vision is presented to her. She does not walk to it, she races towards it!

5) **Uncommon Domain:** her territory and regions are expanded. She is constantly planting and sowing seeds and establishing her areas with authority.

Memorize these so that you counter the little girl (your

inner critic) who shows up to tell you that you aren't necessary! Whoever told you that you weren't enough or made you feel that you weren't needed has a restricted view for a reason. Just because he or she cannot see you, doesn't mean you are less than. It simply means that they are not equipped to see you. They haven't been blessed with supernatural eyes. They are common people with common thoughts. Besides, you have already been confirmed: Yes you are worthy of being seen, having success, and being in loving and fulfilling relationships that feed your spirit! Celebrate that!

I Am A Divine Creation Questions

What does a Divine Creation look like to you?

What do you need to live a life of Unordinary?

Is this the most optimal moment for this need?

What do I need to make this moment a successful moment, one that will meet my need?

What supplies/tools will you need to set yourself up to win?

What habits do you need to discard?

What practices do you need to begin?

What type of support do you need from your tribe? Who are the Divinely appointed people in your life?

What will your future look like when you implement changes?

Tasks/Challenge: Build your Divine Creation List using the Fingerprints of a Supernaturally Made Woman Model. How will you measure your uncommon-ness? What will it look like? Journal about your Divine Encounters or "aha" moments that moved you in your transformation.

Affirmations Just For You!

I Am Necessary

I am Enough

I will be Brave

I Expect Divine Encounters

Use the Affirmations listed above or create some of your own to assist you in your Supernaturally Made journey. Practice repeating them to yourself out loud for one minute. Pay attention to how your attitude and actions. Take it a step further and journal about the changes you notice. Embrace the supernatural person you are becoming and watch the universe open up for you!

ME, ME, I'M FIRST

Chapter 4

How to Get Everything You Want and Enlarge Your Territory

"I'll tell you what Freedom is to me. No Fear."

Nina Simone

Ginger and Civil Rights Activist, Nina Simone understood that if there was any fear among individuals, then freedom could not exist. Nina Simone was undoubtedly a Supernaturally Made Woman. Her statement echoed years ago, during a time when inequality was a regular way of life, pulses loudly through my spirit. It calls me to yell at fear and claim my true position. It challenges my attitude whenever I am in doubt about a new opportunity that the universe blesses me to experience.

Queen, I share this as a testament to what happens when we remove our own imposed restrictions. There is Freedom in asking for what you want. I know this first hand and I want to give you immediate admission too. You have the right of use because of your supernatural status. Your asking does not position you as a vulnerable woman; it positions your heart as a servant. When you do not ask, the universe cannot grant your requests, unless you show up and have a receiver's heart. You must believe that fear has no place in access and it will not prohibit you from getting everything you want

Will you give your vibrant and vivacious self the right to put into practice all of the Supernaturally Made exercises and methods to get everything you want? Your family, business, relationships, career, etc. depend on you applying these principles. If your little girl is fearful right now, then I know your spirit is ready to receive. She is probably kicking and screaming right now telling you to play it safe. I challenge you to ask yourself, "What would life look like if I don't live in freedom?" "What if I don't position myself to get everything I want?" "What if I don't reclaim my Eve?" I sense your urgency and I am geared up to give you access. Are you ready to leap into getting everything you want and enlarging your territory? Kick fear on its butt and propel yourself forward! Deep dive here we come! Use the worksheet at http://www.bit.ly/Imfirst and the tips below to assist you in making decisions that serve you!

Tell your little girl it is okay. You must put your little girl at ease to make big moves. She shows up to protect you and keep you safe. That small fireball of energy needs to know that you have it covered and you do not need her to fight for you at this venture of your journey.

Trust your gut. Your intuition is there for a reason. It is a strong radar. Do not focus on the need to know every answer or know how every situation will turn out.

Be Your Own Endorser. Give yourself permission to ask the universe for everything you want. Your wants turn into honored requests by others when you validate yourself first.

Create a Carte Blanche Lifestyle. Remember you are the Plan A. You have free reign and complete authority to command the life you want. Your checks are all blank and ready for you to cash.

Claim Your Spot in the Universe. What role(s) will you create for yourself? Be free in discovering your purpose. Do not focus on perfection or what others are doing. Your mission is not your competition!

Be Loaded and Lit. Manifestation is important. This is not just a vision board project but also an assertive move in your womanhood renovation. What actions will you take? What actions are necessary to attain your goals? Be an Igniter with your plans and set the world on fire!

Make a Declaration on Reclaiming Your Eve. You are your own evidence and witness to your power to be a woman who lives in and out her purpose. Your position in the world is not contingent on who others say you are or what they want you to be. Stop playing small. Be bold in your declaration and let it overwhelm the world!

How to Get Everything You Want Questions:

What supplies/tools will you need to set yourself up to win?

How will you position your "asks" from the Universe?

What habits do you need to discard?

What practices do you need to begin?

What type of support do you need from your tribe?

What will your future look like when you implement changes?

Tasks/Challenge: Write out your Womanhood Renovation list. This should include things you want to try. Journal how you will operate in fearlessness daily. Write the things you want to become true in your life for the next 90 days and journal about the transformations that have occurred.

Affirmations Just For You!

My Current State is a Temporary Date

I will be Bold In My Requests

I will ask with Certainty Knowing My Requests Will Be Honored

I will let go of being Perfect

Use the Affirmations listed above or create some of your own to assist you in your Supernaturally Made journey. Practice repeating them to yourself out loud for one minute. Pay attention to how your attitude and actions. Take it a step further and journal about the changes you notice. Embrace the supernatural person you are becoming and watch the universe open up for you!

Yes you are worthy of being seen, having success, and being in loving and fulfilling relationships that feed your spirit! Celebrate that!

Chapter 5

You are a Supernatural Investment:
Being a 7-Figure Treasure

Supernaturally Made Woman would not be the treasure she is, without having her financial house in order. This is a part of her responsibility and charge. She makes sure that all domains of her Queendom, especially this area, adequately functions. Think the Proverbs 31 Woman. The more spiritually connected you are to your financial goals will assist you in making wealth driven decisions that serve both you and others.

In my 20's while working in a coveted city position, I was challenged by someone who I will refer to as my "godfather" to make 1 million dollars in 10 years. I call him my godfather, named after the movie "The Godfather." He reminded me of the father in the movie, talking to the son about up leveling the family business and coming up with ways to generate additional revenue. Of course, those words were not used in the movie, but you get where I'm going. I remember my godfather saying, "Sonia you are smart, intelligent, and a go-getter, but you are not going to get rich working in this position. He said, "you own some property, you are single, you make a good salary, but what's next?" What's next? I didn't know I needed a what's next. I made a good salary, could do what I wanted, go where I wanted, and buy what I wanted without a lot of the other considerations that women my age had. I planned to retire in that position!

Up until then I had honestly never thought about making a million dollars or what rich looked like. No one in my family had ever talked about making 1 million dollars. I was taught to go to school, get your degree, and go and get a good job, and ultimately retire. This is the low millionaire mindset. Nobody said anything about up leveling and increasing my revenue, or making a million dollars. None of my girlfriends talked about earning a million dollars nor did my mother, aunts, or female cousins. A million dollars sounded like a lot of money to people. Only rich people had a million dollars. Who said I couldn't have it? There was no law saying I couldn't. But how would I do it? Who was I to dream this big? That little girl showed up again with questions and doubts and I had to immediately silence her. Her conversation was so wrapped up in fear, that I almost laughed at the possibility. I was up for the challenge! My response: "I can do it in 5 years." Now I had to do it!

I have always been an entrepreneur or held an extra stream of income for as long as I can remember. It was how I paid my way through college along with the military's assistance. But how was I going to get to a million dollars? Don't you just love challenges like that, that leave you figuring out the plans? I liked fashion and clothes, so heeding the challenge I begin exploring retailing handbags and perfume along with clothing. This was way before I invested in opening a boutique. The revenue I generated from my part-time retailing allowed me to invest in an actual storefront where I sold wellness products in addition to the clothing and accessories.

Investing in the boutique was the best move I have ever done, even until this day. It allowed me to really learn how to operate and run a business and it provided a blueprint for the future and it drove how I would invest in other businesses which ultimately allowed me to accomplish the 1 million dollars challenge in 5 years!

That "good paying" job I had? I lost it. Lucky for me I had designed a 7-figure financial plan that sustained my lifestyle and could be repeated in other businesses, well before I ever started coaching. I know use this blueprint to help other women in my 7 Figure Treasure Financial Series Workshops that I conduct quarterly. https://www.eventbrite.com/e/you-are-a-7-figure-treasure-financial-mindset-series-for-women-tickets-41229534648

I share my story not to brag, but because I believe it is essential that women consistently talk about money among other women. We need to support each other in our financial goals. We need to root for each other every time one of us accomplishes a goal or achieves a major win. No longer can we allow each other to function from a place of "lack." When we conduct financial matters in a mindset of lack, we allow our fears and insecurities about money to direct our actions. This is direct connection with the messages we receive as women about money that are rooted in culture, economics, and religious standards. Unfortunately, this shapes our financial blueprint about money and positions us to operate from an attitude of scarcity, which causes us back away from being good financial managers and wealth builders. Discussions about finances and our approach from both a financial and spiritual realm therefore are necessary. They both operate together to confirm you as a 7-Figure Treasure.

How does a Supernaturally Made Woman become a 7-Figure Treasure? Take a look below at some characteristics. These are the practices that I used to assist me in developing my 7-Figure Treasure Blueprint. Please try them and share with other women!

Characteristics of a 7-Figure Treasure:

- She is a Supernatural Investor. She sets both her financial and spiritual goals to be in service to her family, herself, and others.

- She initiates and takes action. She creates opportunities to increase her wealth.

- She allows others to contribute to who she is. She looks to her network of friends and supporters to assist her in accumulating wealth.

- She is industrious and proactive. She looks at all actions and possibilities to plan for future earnings and spending. She utilizes her resources to support her in her wealth building goals and results.

- She invests and uses her time wisely. She monetizes her value. She does her research to either invest in herself as a business or a product that will generate an investment.

- She places a value on her contributions. She is aware that her gifts and service are of high value and deserves compensation.

- She knows that she is a wealth builder. Her intelligence is her biggest capital. She uses her brain to create opportunities for long-term revenue.

- She creates a circle of people who add value, connect and aid her in expanding her Queendom.

- She uses her expertise, skills and experience to create value. These transactions transfer into wealth building.

- She stays away from the low millionaire mindset. She operates in fullness while avoiding conversations and spaces that focus on lack.

- She operates from a servant's heart. She shares her gifts with the world. She understands that the more she gives, more is given back to her.

- She applies the values of prosperity. When she gives, she grows. When she grows, she gives.

- She does not have any emotional energy around money. She understands that money is a natural resource and used to do good, give back, etc.

The 7-Figure Treasure Mindset Questions

What is my attitude about money?

What messages did you receive about money culturally spiritually?

How did this shape your view?

What supplies/tools will you need to set yourself up to win?

What financial habits do you need to discard?

What financial practices do you need to begin?

What type of support do you need from your tribe?

What will your future look like when you implement changes?

Tasks/Challenge: Using the Characteristics of a 7-Figure Treasure create a list or plan that reflects your goals both financially and spiritually. Implement your creation and follow your plan for 30 days. Journal your progress and transformations.

Affirmations Just For You!

Use the Affirmations listed below or create some of your own to assist you in your Supernaturally Made journey. Practice repeating them to yourself out loud for one minute. Pay attention to how your attitude and actions. Take it a step further and journal about the changes you notice. Embrace the supernatural person you are becoming and watch the universe open up for you!

I am a Powerful Creator

Money is Effortless

I will make my Ask Big

I will expect, believe, and receive big

I Am an Opportunity Magnet

You are a product of a divine creation based on your lineage and connection to Eve. If she was the one and only plan, then so are you.

Chapter 6

Supernatural Success:

Mindset Principles for the Supernatural Woman

"The Future I want is one where I can do the most good."

Dr. Sonia Kennedy

You were planned. A beautiful, premeditated plan, called to make a difference in the world and to live purposefully. As a Supernaturally Made Woman, how we govern ourselves in the world is important. This starts with a mindset guided by what I call, The Supernatural Success Manifesto. These are guiding principles that every woman should incorporate into her everyday lifestyle for her supernatural success.

If you are Supernaturally Made, then you will be Supernaturally Successful in your life! Supernatural Success principles are based on energy, expectation, being intentional and deliberate about life choices, expressing gratitude, and submitting your requests to the Universe. They stop you from operating out of habit or out of presence and focus. In this chapter, I will cover a few distinct points from the Supernatural Success Manifesto that I created and routinely use in my coaching practice with my clients and women leaders. I want to position you to begin to lead deliberately and powerfully in your homes, at work, in your businesses, and in your relationships.

The **<u>Supernatural Success Manifesto Directives</u>** listed below are in no specific order. Apply them throughout the day as you encounter challenging or confusing situations.

Create an Empowered Mission and Purpose. Your goal is to live a full life, to gain knowledge, and impart wisdom among other women and those in need of your supernatural energy.

Appreciate the Life Journey. Create a space for self-compassion and mistakes. Turn your teachable moments into knowledge. Take your knowledge and make it wisdom that you share with others.

Build a Space/Container that Holds You. Get still. When you are uncertain, use the knowledge and information you have to determine next steps.

Be Intentionally Successful. When you are intentional, you live your life on purpose and live it out purposefully. You are in charge and called to make a difference.

Own Your Truth. Who you are as a Supernaturally Made Woman revolves around your truth and the stories you tell yourself and others. If you tell a negative story, you become that story.

Embrace who you are. Be authentic and transparent about who you are. Let go of who you think you are supposed to be.

Build an Empowered Body. A Supernaturally Made Woman will focus on her physical health as a form of self-care. She will commit to incorporating a physical fitness routine into her daily activities. She will make better food choices that nurture her energy.

Operate in Gratitude. A Supernaturally Made Woman understands the spiritual practice of gratitude in every aspect of her life and she expresses her gratitude openly to manifest her dreams.

Supernatural Success Mindset Questions:

What do you need to live purposefully?

Is this the most optimal moment for this need?

What do I need to make this moment a successful moment, one that will meet my need?

What supplies/tools will you need to set yourself up to win?

What habits do you need to discard?

What practices do you need to begin?

What type of support do you need from your tribe?

What will your future look like when you implement changes?

Tasks/Challenges: Using the principles of the Supernatural Success Manifesto, create your own Supernatural Success Manifesto. What will it include? How will the manifesto serve you? What beliefs and values will you incorporate?

Affirmations Just For You!

Use the Affirmations listed below or create some of your own to assist you in your Supernaturally Made journey. Practice repeating them to yourself out loud for one minute. Pay attention to how your attitude and actions. Take it a step further and journal about the changes you notice. Embrace the supernatural person you are becoming and watch the universe open up for you!

I am Supernaturally Made

My Time is Now

I will serve in Humility

I will operate in Gratitude

Chapter 7

Self-Love and Emotional Empowerment for the Supernatural Woman

Now is the time to stop feeling guilty and hesitant, about taking care of you. It is a necessary must. It is awesome to be blessed to be a supernatural woman. I do not want you to ever doubt that or your calling to be an agent. You know where you come from and to whom you belong. You understand that your gifts are valuable to the world, thus, you need to be proactive instead of reactive in how you love on yourself. You can be both a work in progress (growing) as well as a masterpiece (purposeful).

How you take care of you is non-negotiable. It is necessary that you do this. Do not just try to blow through it or "man up". You are created as woman, not a man. No need to put on shoes that you know will not fit. Shoes that are too tight hurt. If they are too big, we struggle to fill them and keep them on our feet. As a consequence of wearing the wrong shoes, our ability to be introspective is minimized. We do not have time to be in a reflective state. Give yourself permission to be still or to cry, or better yet to be angry. If we are emotional creatures, then why is not okay for us to express our emotions without being made to feel ashamed or guilty?

Embrace your talents and strengths, but do not use these as a measure of performance or comparison to the mainstream culture of perfection. You know the culture of today's woman: the hustling, grinding, making-it-happen mentality, who is constantly try to measure up, all the while neglecting her self-care? Sis, can we have a real conversation on getting back to loving you? Can we just sit for a moment and do a me-flection so we can dialogue and get an understanding about the mixed messages of being a go-getter? We want to get things done and focus on your self-care as a pathway to emotional empowerment. Can we do that? I am so ready for this conversation with you. Grab your favorite beverage, your journal, pen, and a highlighter and let us unpack this together.

I want to tell you, and reiterate author Suzanne Burden's statement, **"The world desperately needs you!"** Let that marinate for a minute. Yes, woman, diva, Supreme Goddess, & Queen, the world needs you in it! It cannot function without you. It is just that simple. I will let you in on another secret: it is okay to let the world center around you. No, for real, you can place yourself in a position of receivership from the world. You deserve to be served too! Contrary to the messages we receive, it is okay to be at the center of attention and be nurtured by the world. Author, motivational speaker, and clergywoman, Karri Turner, attests to this in her book, *The Girl Bible.* Turner, states that many women have heard the adage, "the world does not revolve around you." She differs with that opinion and suggests that the world does revolve around women in that we are "directly responsible for what does and does not manifest in your [our] life." I vibe with this because what Karri is talking about is the power and control that women give up first and in my opinion too easy.

In Chapter 2, **Rocking Your Queendom: You Are A Woman of Unique Distinction,** I talked to you about being the Plan A. This is applicable to your self-care as well. You are a part of the A Team, built with a design in mind to create the world. This was all in God's plan as He created. He knew the purpose for which He created you. No births could happen, the world could not be populated without you, and we would not have so many brilliant and strong women in the world without you. You, my Queen, are the essential design in the master plan of the world. Therefore, you must take care of yourself. The world is depending on you to be present!

Self-Love & Emotional Empowerment Questions:

What are some actions that you can take to nurture you?

What supplies/tools will you need to set yourself up to win?

What habits do you need to discard?

What self-care practices do you need to begin?

What type of support do you need from your tribe?

What physical movements or actions will you incorporate?

What will your future look like when you implement changes?

Tasks/Challenges: Create your list of Emotional Empowerment. How will you honor yourself? Does your list include forgiveness? What boundaries will you set to protect your self-care? Include a self-care plan that involves physical movement and rewards to yourself.

Affirmations Just For You!

Use the Affirmations listed below or create some of your own to assist you in your Supernaturally Made journey. Practice repeating them to yourself out loud for one minute. Pay attention to how your attitude and actions. Take it a step further and journal about the changes you notice. Embrace the supernatural person you are becoming and watch the universe open up for you!

I will forgive myself

I will not live in Shame

I will practice healthy self-talk filled with love for me

Chapter 8

Your Identity as a Supernatural Individual

"I am Not Afraid of Taking Risks, No one Can Define Me"

Beyoncé

"You can't heal what you won't face." I remember hearing this from author and world renowned life coach, Iyanla Vanzant. This is a powerful and true statement that warrants our immediate attention regarding who we are, if we want to have continuous growth in our goal of transformation. ***In Chapter 2: Rocking Your Queendom: You are a Unique Woman of Distinction,*** I ask you to claim you queendom as a Plan A. Now let's explore how old issues show up to challenge the new womanhood journey that you are creating!

Many of us, at some time or another have faced issues or had experiences with fear, rejection, and self-doubt that shape who we are-positively or negatively. Depending on our response to these experiences, our identities are bound in conflict: we either show up in the world with (a) limiting beliefs that restrict our growth and potential or (b) we operate behind masks: accomplishments, looks, or performance which leaves the person continually desiring success but avoiding failure. This is one of the symptoms of the perfectionism syndrome label.

In my coaching practice with my business clients, many of them struggle with these same issues. Although they show up as high achievers to others, their power to reach their full potential is controlled by the identity that they have claimed and by their internal pain that has been left unaddressed. I work with my clients to help them overcome perfectionism syndrome by doing a deep exploration of self as it relates to both their business and personal development! We examine who they are and what they need to let go for them to launch their businesses or for their businesses to flourish. I then assist them in reframing their stories so that the old messages and identities are positioned to allow them to tell a new story of success! Often, this work is intense for some of my clients, but I strongly believe in the saying: "How you show up in your personal life, is how you show up in your business!"

As a supernaturally made individual you have the power to unleash your gifts so that you can have an awesome personal life or thriving business. You were created to be the answer on the planet! You don't have to wait on the call to be chosen, the call was already made!

Because you have already been called, you don't have to compare yourself to anyone else or pick yourself apart based on what others are doing. You don't have to make stuff look pretty. You are supernaturally made to create any reality you want for yourself. It can be as big and as fabulous as you want it to be! You can be clear about who you are and what you are in your personal life or business. How? I know that it is possible to have what you want, because I have done it through a visualization process called Imagineering. When I first started my coaching business, I used this to help me visualize and meditate on the future that I wanted to create.

I visualized myself writing, serving others, traveling, speaking, even shopping and purchasing the designer shoes that I wanted. A girl has to include shopping in her dreams, right? And you know what? All those things happened! All because I was in a mindset of receivership and connection. This is a practice that I do daily. It helps me to continuously disable any previous negative programming and create from a place of power and possibility. Now, this process isn't just for me! It is available for everyone to utilize. You too can create a receivership process for yourself that is filled with abundance. When you practice this, you will see your world open up with opportunities!

Supernatural Success Identity Questions:

What do you need to own your identity?

Is this the most optimal moment for this need?

What do I need to make my moments be full of success and ones that will meet my need?

What supplies/tools will you need to set yourself up to win?

What habits do you need to discard?

What practices do you need to begin?

What type of support do you need from your tribe?

What will your future look like when you implement changes?

Affirmations Just For You!

Use the Affirmations listed below or create some of your own to assist you in your Supernaturally Made journey. Practice repeating them to yourself out loud for one minute. Pay attention to how your attitude and actions. Take it a step further and journal about the changes you notice. Embrace the supernatural person you are becoming and watch the universe open up for you!

I am Worthy of My Desires

I have all of the tools within me to achieve Success

I Envision My Life Positively

Embrace your talents and strengths, but do not use these as a measure of performance or comparison to the mainstream culture of perfection.

Chapter 9

Perfectly Imperfect:
Challenges of the Supernatural Woman

"We must confess that we are the possible."

Maya Angelou

We all make mistakes in our personal lives as well as in business. The key to growth and success in either area is to keep moving towards your goal. We improve because we do things imperfectly. Mistakes are never final. For example, think about a person that you admire. Imagine if you had the opportunity to ask them the kind of mistakes that they have made? What do you think they would say? Would it be all positives? Negatives? A combination of both?

How do you see mistakes? Is it through "trial and error" or from a mentality of "I can learn from my mistakes?" Which way of thinking is more helpful for you? Do you think you should make mistakes? I believe that we should make mistakes. It makes us take more risks and build confidence in trying something new. If you believe you shouldn't make mistakes, then you will take less risks or infrequently try something new. This also leads to avoidance of doing things that may feel uncomfortable.

If you were to implement all of the practices of a Supernaturally Made Woman from Chapters 1-8 would you aim for perfection or would you look at your journey-as you making progress daily? The goal of a Supernaturally Made Woman is always progress, not perfection!

Mistakes are our learning experiences that give us the opportunity to learn and improve. Do not think about winning each time you set out to complete a goal. If you never lose, then you can't learn how to win.

We all have flaws that make us unique. Some people just do better at covering up their imperfections versus others. The flaws are our supernatural ability to accomplish great things. If you make a mistake, take another chance. If you make another mistake, take a chance again. There is no moratorium on making mistakes or rules that say after 3 tries you are out!

Give yourself permission to do things imperfectly each time you try or learn a new skill. No criticism allowed. You will have more accomplishments because of your attempts that will ultimately you will get to your goal.

Supernatural Success Perfection Questions:

What do you need to give yourself permission to make mistakes?

Is this the most optimal moment for this need?

What do I need to make this moment a successful moment, one that will meet my need?

What supplies/tools will you need to set yourself up to win?

What habits do you need to discard?

What practices do you need to begin?

What type of support do you need from your tribe?

What will your future look like when you implement changes?

Affirmations Just For You!

Use the Affirmations listed below or create some of your own to assist you in your Supernaturally Made journey. Practice repeating them to yourself out loud for one minute. Pay attention to how your attitude and actions. Take it a step further and journal about the changes you notice. Embrace the supernatural person you are becoming and watch the universe open up for you!

I am Perfectly Imperfect

I will be Compassionate with Myself

I will Practice Self-Acceptance

Bonus Chapter:

From the new book: The Superpower Playbook: 7 Ways to Unleash The Power Within, Supernaturally Made Vol. 2

Superheroes are Improvers: Building Intentional Relationships with Others

"Please take my hand. I give it to you as a gesture of friendship and love."-Wonder Woman

By now your superpower toolbox should be quite full and it may be a lot of information to absorb! Remember you are in a position of a learner. So allow yourself some room to learn! If your are excited and ready to apply some of the tools that you have learned so far, go right ahead. Let me know how you are doing too!

Relationships play an important role in all of our lives. Superheroes don't always operate in isolation. Every superhero belonged to some form of organization or community, The Justice League, The Avengers, and The X-Men are prime examples. They recognize the power of connection and community in improving and advancing mankind's progress. Professor X, of the X-men comes to mind. He taught other superheroes to believe in a future where all humans/mutants would come together and improve their relationships, united in the fight for peace and equality. As a superhero, you have the same responsibility to create relationships and teach others how to create authentic connections. This is essential for your future plans. When we make connections and improve upon our relationships with others we create community and build upon our knowledge.

Here are some quick tools and practices to develop your Superpower as an Improver:

Superheroes are resilient. Call upon your inner efficacy to adjust easily from any setbacks. Setbacks are temporary states designed to teach a lesson.

Superheroes are optimistic. Operate from a space hopefulness and confidence about the future.

Superheroes are able to tolerate uncertainty. Be open to accepting change.

Superheroes are critical thinkers. You must put the time in to generate ideas based on your vision and synthesize information.

Superheroes are team players. You put aside your personal goals and work to help others, doing what you need to do to strive for a common goal.

Superheroes use a form of systems thinking to make meaning of the world. Be willing to explore different ways of doing things.

Superheroes are connection makers. You must be willing to embrace the wisdom of the crowds and believe in the power of community.

Superheroes are questioners. Explore not what works, but what works, for who and under what set of conditions in your business and life.

Superheroes are problem finders. What problem are you trying to solve? What has worked before?

Superheroes are reflective. Be ready and open to learning and understanding of self. Look at lessons from experience. Remember lessons learned aren't necessarily mistakes. You are also looking at what worked well.

Superheroes are facilitators. Make actions and processes easy when you are teaching or leading. Don't forget the goal is to empower others to go out and take action!

Superheroes are willing to fail. Leave room for failure. That failure may occur is not the problem, failing to learn is!

Building relationships don't just happen by accident. It is done through effort and process. Using your superpower as an improver means that you go beyond just one single outcome in building relationships! Helping others have a BYOB moment is a bonus!

(BYOB): Quick Superhero Activity: To get you in action using your superpower and the playbook, try this activity:

Want to improve your relationships or business? Elevate your social environment by actively seeking out success-minded people who are willing to be in a reciprocal relationship.

Appendix A

Supernatural Tools To Use

Use the tools on the next 3 pages to assist you in your journey as a Supernaturally Made Woman. There are no wrong answers for the exercises. This is a space for your reflections, thoughts, and ideas. Have fun, release, and explore!

Supernaturally Made: Abundance Practice

Make a list of everything your desire. Create a space for yourself where you write a list of everything that you desire. Make sure your space is a representation of you, beautiful, courageous, and inspiring. When you make your list, make sure that you are alone and its quiet. Put candles in your space and bring your favorite tea, wine, or other beverage. Close your eyes and inhale a few breaths through your nose. As you exhale out through your mouth, visualize positive things happening for you and to you. Take a few more breaths so that you can get a clear picture in your mind of what you want your life to look life. As you exhale again, release any negative or fearful thoughts. When writing your list say your supernatural affirmations that you created. Tell yourself you can have everything you want! That your dreams are not too big! That you are Supernaturally Made and there are no limits!

Making Room For Imperfections

Think about a situation in your life or business that challenged you. Was it a stressful day, a difficult client, or an idea that didn't go as planned. What did you learn from that situation? How did that situation help you grow?

Making Mistakes

How do you think about mistakes? Take a minute to answer the questions below as they apply to you, then write about why you choose the answers.

If I make a mistake, I think I am a failure

If I make a mistake I think I can never learn

If I make a mistake I think I should give up

I think I shouldn't make mistakes

If I make a mistake I think I am human—everyone makes mistakes

If I make a mistake I think I am in the process of learning

If I make a mistake I think I can try harder and persist and keep going

If I make a mistake, I remind myself that I should make mistakes—no one is perfect, especially me

Thoughts:
_____
_____
_____
_____
_____

Congratulations Beauty! You did it! Your Supernaturally Made Transformation is in effect. You showed up, stepped out, and did a full 360. I hope this book has empowered you to claim your true purpose in the world! I hope that you feel more confident about who you are and know both in heart and mind how valuable and important you are! You are the Plan A!

What's next now that you have this life of a Supernaturally Made Woman? I want you to dive into this work you have started so that you can stay on track on this forever journey. You can do this with my new **Supernaturally Made book, Vol. 2: "The Superpower Playbook: 7 Ways to Unleash Your Power Within"** **available on amazon.com.**

A huge thank you for letting me take this journey with you! I want you to let me know how you are doing. What new ideas and plans have you created after reading Supernaturally Made, Vol. 1? Any uncommon thoughts or actions? I am looking for Supernaturally Made Ambassadors to create a tsunami and show up big in the world! Send me your thoughts and ideas for my future books, blog, and podcasts @ http://www.drsoniakennedy@empoweringwellness360.com. I want to hear from you!

I pray that this book was of benefit to you and those around you with whom you shared this book. Change is ongoing and a part of your larger process. Anyone making it look easy, is not being transparent. Your Womanhood Renovation depends on you and how you resist the notions of perfection, live your life purposely, and show up for yourself each and every day. It will get challenging at times but remember-you are Supernaturally Made and a Plan A! Do not ever forget that!

Bonus Offer! To show my profound gratitude for your support

I am inviting my readers and community to a **FREE** Supernatural Success 30-minute Coaching call. This call can be used for either personal development or business coaching! The call will be laser focused to help you get clarity and take action! You can schedule your **FREE** session at http://www.bit.ly/powerpusher.

ABOUT THE AUTHOR

Dr. Sonia Kennedy is an Author, Success Coach, Speaker, & Visionary Leadership Trainer. As a Licensed Clinical Therapist, Researcher, and Certified Yoga Instructor, Dr. Sonia works with clients to transform and ignite their mindsets, unleash their supernatural powers, show up fabulously, and get healthy, all while creating a life worth celebrating!

Dr. Sonia believes in the power of a person's journey and the transformational story that unfolds. Her goal is to use those stories to empower individuals to unlock their mental blocks and help clients align their vision with their lifestyle goals. Whether you want to gain clarity, self-awareness, lose weight, or re-align your business, career, financial, and organizational goals, Dr. Sonia assists you in **"UPPING"** your life and taking action. A primary part of the work with Dr. Sonia is **helping clients who want to have a (BYOB) moment: Beyond Your Ordinary Best!**

Let's talk! I would love to hear from you! Tell me your story and share it in the next Supernaturally Made Book!

I am available to speak and host at conferences and

workshops. Want to stay up to date on the next Supernatural Success Workshop and latest events? You can sign up for the Supernaturally Made newsletter on my blog at http://www.bit.ly.getyouryes.

Help build the Supernaturally Made community on my Instagram page @YogaBodhi360. You can also follow me on my personal page at facebook.com/soniakennedy. Don't forget to take advantage of the **FREE** 30-minute Supernatural Success laser focused coaching call! May your journey be successful and prosperous! Feel free to email me at or via my website at http://www.empoweringwellness360.com.

www.ingramcontent.com/pod-product-compliance
Lightning Source LLC
Chambersburg PA
CBHW071230160426
43196CB00012B/2464